BookLife PUBLISHING

©2021
BookLife Publishing Ltd.
King's Lynn
Norfolk PE30 4LS

ISBN: 978-1-83927-491-6

Written by:
William Anthony

Edited by:
Robin Twiddy

Designed by:
Amy Li

All rights reserved. Printed in Malta.

A catalogue record for this book is available from the British Library.

All facts, statistics, web addresses and URLs in this book were verified as valid and accurate at time of writing. No responsibility for any changes to external websites or references can be accepted by either the author or publisher.

Photo Credits

Images are courtesy of Shutterstock.com. With thanks to Getty Images, Thinkstock Photo and iStockphoto.

Recurring images – ONYXprj (builders), Elenamiv, sidmay (blue background), Guiyuan Chen (wood background), art4stock (push pins), ag1100 (crumpled paper). Cover – LightField Studios, p4–5 – Nina Buday, p6–7 – Nolte Lourens, Maria-Cezara Panaite, Rawpixel.com, Sergiy Bykhunenko, p8–9 – KK Tan, p10–11 – Glinskaja Olga, mimagephotography, SnvvSnvvSnvv, Impact Photography, p12–13 – Tropper, p14–15 – Dmitry Lobanov, Hryshchyshen Serhii, PV productions, p16–17 – MIA Studio, p18–19 – Sorbis, Dean Drobot, Anatoliy Karlyuk, Katt_Parrot.

Local Area BUILDERS

Contents

Page 4	Meet the Local Area Builders!
Page 6	Clothes Shop
Page 10	Arts and Crafts Shop
Page 14	Supermarket
Page 18	Toy Shop
Page 20	Our Local Area
Page 22	Your Local Area
Page 24	Glossary and Index

Words that look like <u>this</u> can be found in the glossary on page 24.

Meet the Local Area Builders

Hello! We're the Local Area Builders. We help <u>communities</u> by building important things in their local area. This map is quite empty, isn't it? Someone will need somewhere to shop soon, I'm sure!

New Building Needed:
Something for Fashion

I want to go shopping for clothes, but there's nowhere to go! I love <u>fashion</u> and dressing in the coolest clothes. Can we build a clothes shop?

– Jamie, aged 6

That didn't take long! Let's get going on our first job!

Clothes Shop

A clothes shop is where people go to buy the things they wear. In a clothes shop, you could buy dresses, shirts, shoes or even a funky hat.

I love wearing bright clothes to stand out!

In a shop, we use <u>money</u> to buy things.

I like smart clothes best of all!

Many people wear different <u>styles</u> of clothing. Every style is different and great in its own way. Whatever style you like is great if it makes you happy!

Map Update

That clothes shop will keep everyone looking great! I think we should build two or three clothes shops, so there are lots of styles to choose from.

Clothes shops

New Building Needed: Something Arty

I love painting, drawing and making things — anything to do with art! But I have run out of paint and paper! Could we build a shop where I could get these things?

— Sara, aged 5

 Of course we can. Let's get building!

Arts and Crafts Shop

An arts and crafts shop is a place where you can buy <u>materials</u> for art <u>projects</u>. You can buy things such as paper, pencils, paint, glue and many more arty things!

I can make lots of different things by folding paper. It is called origami.

Art can be a fun <u>hobby</u>. What hobbies do you have?

I paint how I feel. If I'm happy, I use bright colours!

Art can be anything you want it to be. It might be a dot on a page, a swirl of colours or a big painting of someone's face. All art is different and good.

Map Update

This place is going to look amazing! An arts and crafts shop will help people with their hobbies. Maybe we could even have an art show one day!

Arts and crafts shop

New Building Needed: Something for Food

Cooking is one of my favourite hobbies. It's fun to do, and when you're done you get a tasty treat! I need somewhere to get <u>ingredients</u>. Can you help?

—Ben, aged 5

This is making my tummy rumble. Let's build something, quick!

Supermarket

I like the bit with all the sweets! Who wouldn't?

A supermarket is a shop where you can buy all kinds of food, from vegetables to sweets. Supermarkets are normally very big shops.

Always stay with an adult when you visit a supermarket. It is easy to get lost!

Supermarkets don't just sell food. They sometimes sell things like birthday cards, <u>stationery</u> and video games.

Map Update

New Building Needed: Something Fun

Toys are the best. They are the best of the best. But there's nowhere in the local area where I can get new ones! Can we build somewhere fun?

— Cho, aged 5

This should have been the first shop we built! Let's get going!

Toy Shop

Toy shops are full of fun and wonder. They are packed with toys, games, puzzles and much more. Toy shops might have new toys or toys from many years ago.

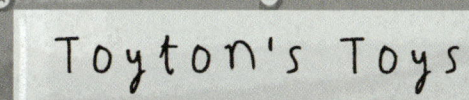

Toyton's Toys

Dolls are great because you can act out stories with them.

I love doing puzzles because they are a challenge.

Some toy shops have toys that you can try out in the shop. The people that work there might show you how a toy works and let you play with it.

Our Local Area

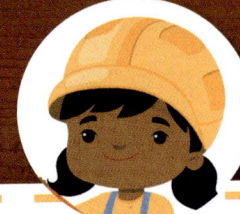

That toy shop will give us kids a place to have loads of fun! The map looks much better now. Maybe one day we could build a big shopping centre.

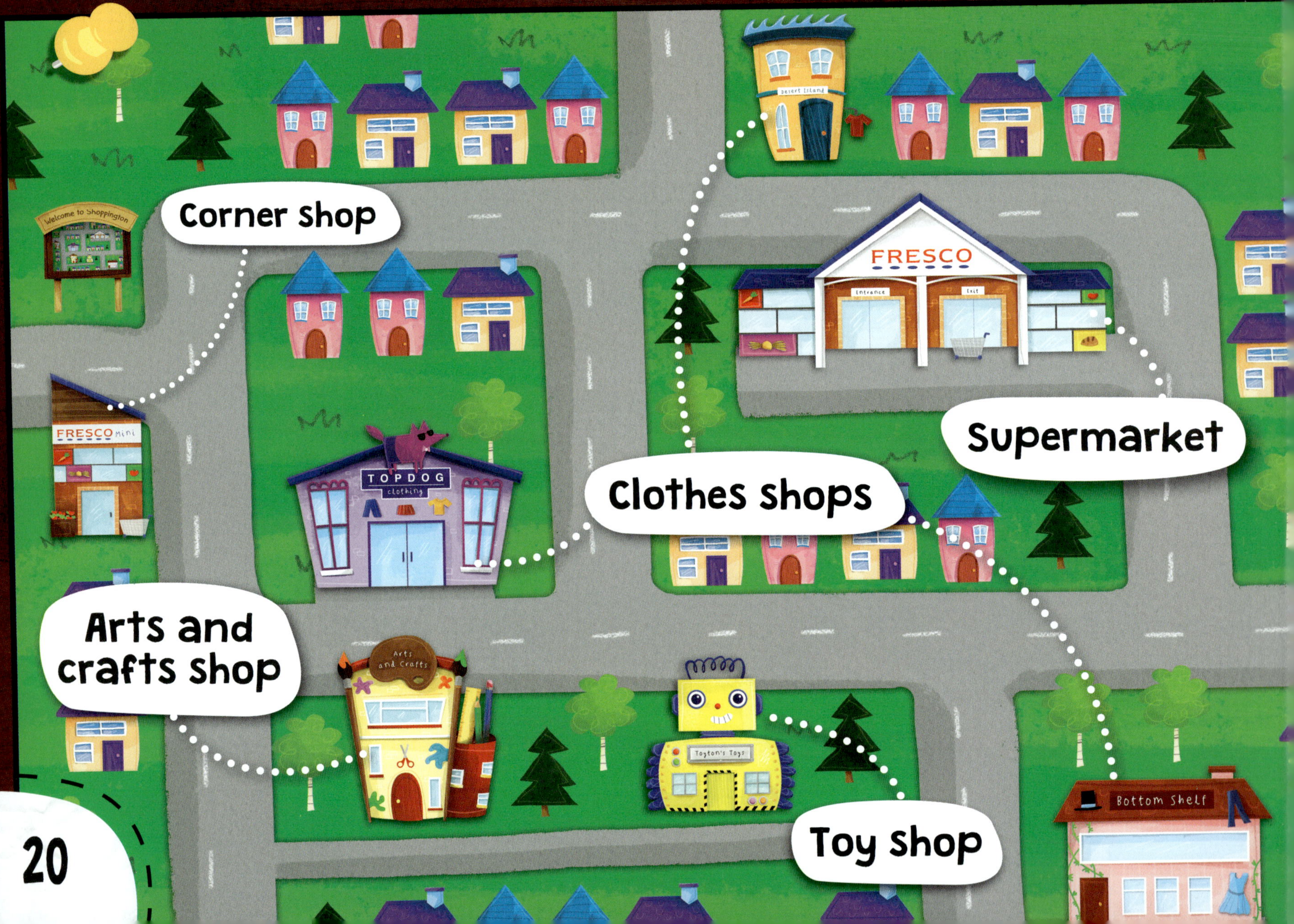

Corner shop
FRESCO
Supermarket
FRESCO mini
TOPDOG
Clothes shops
Arts and crafts shop
Toy shop
Bottom Shelf

Our work here is finished. This local area has lots of places to buy things and explore different hobbies. It's time to go and build somewhere else. Great job, everybody!

Welcome to Shoppington

Your Local Area

It's time to try creating a local area yourself! Grab a piece of paper and draw an empty map like the one on page 4.

What's in your local area? Are there toy shops and supermarkets?

Edible bakery

Think about your local area. Draw all the places where you can buy something on your map. Or you could make one up and go completely bonkers! It's up to you!

What's in your made-up local area? What about a shop made from sweets or a place you can buy a pet dinosaur?

Glossary

communities	groups of people who live and work in the same place
fashion	a popular way of dressing
hobby	an activity that somebody does for fun
ingredients	things that are used to make food
materials	things from which objects are made
money	something used to pay for things
projects	something that requires careful work over a long time
shopping centre	group of shops in one area, sometimes in a very large building
stationery	things that are used for writing or drawing
styles	ways that people are dressed

Index

art 9–12, 20
clothes 5–8, 20
communities 4
food 13–16
hobbies 11–13, 21
toys 17–20, 22